Gone Forever!
Iguanodon

Rupert Matthews

Heinemann
LIBRARY

www.heinemann.co.uk/library
Visit our website to find out more information about Heinemann Library books.

To order:

Phone ++44 (0)1865 888066

Send a fax to ++44 (0)1865 314091

Visit the Heinemann Bookshop at www.heinemann.co.uk/library to browse our catalogue and order online.

First published in Great Britain by Heinemann Library, Halley Court, Jordan Hill, Oxford OX2 8EJ, a part of Harcourt Education. Heinemann is a registered trademark of Harcourt Education Ltd.

Editorial: Andrew Farrow and Dan Nunn
Design: Ron Kamen and Paul Davies and Associates
Illustrations: James Field of Simon Girling and Associates
Picture Research: Rebecca Sodergren and Ginny Stroud-Lewis
Production: Viv Hichens
Originated by Ambassador Litho Ltd
Printed and bound in China by South China Printing Company

07 06 05 04 03
10 9 8 7 6 5 4 3 2 1
ISBN 0 431 16616 1

British Library Cataloguing in Publication Data
Matthews, Rupert
Iguanodon. - (Gone forever)
1. Iguanodon - Juvenile literature
I. Title
567.9'14

Acknowledgements
The Publishers are grateful to the following for permission to reproduce copyright material: Museum of Brussels, Belgium p. **22**; Natural History Museum, London pp. **4, 6, 8, 10, 12, 13, 18, 20, 24, 26**; Science Photo Library p. **16**; Senekenberg Nature Museum/DK p. **14**.

Cover photo reproduced with permission of the Natural History Museum, London.

Our thanks to Dr Angela Milner of the Natural History Museum, London for her assistance in the preparation of this book.

Every effort has been made to contact copyright holders of any material reproduced in this book. Any omissions will be rectified in subsequent printings if notice is given to the Publishers.

Disclaimer

All the Internet addresses (URLs) given in this book were valid at the time of going to press. However, due to the dynamic nature of the Internet, some addresses may have changed, or sites may have ceased to exist since publication. While the author and Publishers regret any inconvenience this may cause readers, no responsibility for any such changes can be accepted by either the author or the Publishers.

Contents

Some words are shown in bold, **like this**.
You can find out what they mean by looking in the Glossary.

Gone forever!

Some animals become **extinct**. This means that all the animals of that type die out. None are left alive anywhere. Scientists can find out about these extinct animals by studying **fossils**.

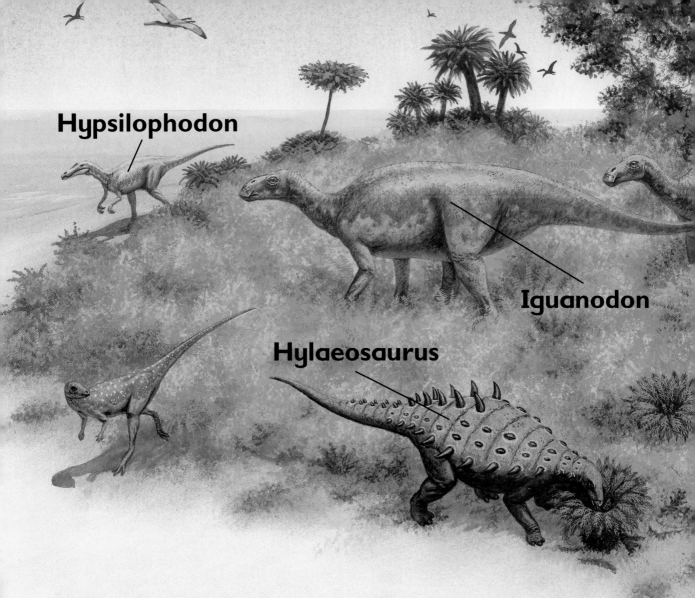

Hypsilophodon

Iguanodon

Hylaeosaurus

Iguanodon is an extinct animal. It lived about 120 million years ago in many places around the world. It was a plant-eating **dinosaur**. The dinosaurs and nearly all other animals that lived at the time of Iguanodon have also become extinct.

Iguanodon's home

Scientists called **geologists** study rocks. They look at the rocks in which Iguanodon **fossils** have been found. These rocks can tell scientists about the place where Iguanodon lived.

teeth

rocks containing
Iguanodon teeth

The land where Iguanodon lived was warm. There was plenty of rain. There were low hills and a few **valleys** with rivers running through them. Most of the land was covered by forests, but there was also some open land. Many Iguanodon fossils have been found in areas that used to be **marshes**.

Changing plants

Scientists have found **fossil** plants in the same rocks as fossils of Iguanodon. This meant that they grew when Iguanodon was alive. One of the plants was a type of plant that had never grown before. This was a plant with flowers.

fossil leaf of an early flowering plant

Before the time of Iguanodon, none of the plants on Earth had flowers. The first plants with flowers were small and grew in damp places in **valleys**. Today plants with flowers grow all over the world.

Other dinosaurs

**Polacanthus
armour plates**

Fossils of other **dinosaurs** have been found in
the same rocks as the fossils of Iguanodon. One
of these dinosaurs was Polacanthus. Scientists
have found fewer fossils of Polacanthus than of
Iguanodon. This means it was probably not as
common as Iguanodon.

10

Polacanthus was about four metres long. It ate the leaves and shoots of plants near the ground. It had large spikes and tough bone **armour** along its back. These gave it protection against meat-eating dinosaurs.

Getting it wrong

Fossils of Iguanodon were some of the very first **dinosaur** bones ever found. At first, only some teeth were found. Then people discovered some leg bones, a thumb spike and a few ribs. Scientists were not sure how the bones fitted together.

In 1854, scientists built a model of what they thought Iguanodon looked like. They thought it was like a rhinoceros! Many more fossils have now been found. Now we know what it really looked like!

What was Iguanodon?

Scientists called **palaeontologists** study the **fossils** of **dinosaurs** such as Iguanodon. They find out what the dinosaur looked like and how it lived. They know a lot about Iguanodon because so many fossils have been found.

14

Iguanodon was up to ten metres long. It weighed up to five tonnes. Its teeth show us that Iguanodon ate plants. The bones show it was very strong and could move quite quickly.

Baby Iguanodon

Scientists have not found any Iguanodon eggs or any **fossils** of babies. But perhaps young Iguanodon **hatched** from eggs laid in nests of mud and leaves. The young were probably about 35 centimetres long when they hatched.

dinosaur eggs

The babies may have stayed in the nest for several weeks. The mother Iguanodon probably brought them food to eat. When the young were large enough to look after themselves, they left the nest.

On the move

The **hind** legs of Iguanodon were strong and **muscular** with three toes. The front legs had feet with five toes. Three of the toes ended in small **hooves**. Iguanodon may have rested on its front legs when bending down to drink or to eat small plants.

an Iguanodon hind foot

18

Iguanodon probably walked on all fours most of the time. This way of walking does not use much **energy**. Iguanodon could stand up on its hind legs to reach food. It could also look around in case meat-eating **dinosaurs** were near.

Run for it!

The **hind** legs of Iguanodon were long and strong. The bones show that powerful **muscles** joined the legs to the hips. Iguanodon could move using just its hind legs.

20

Scientists think Iguanodon ran on its hind legs when it wanted to move quickly. It could run if it was attacked. Iguanodon could probably escape from a powerful meat-eating **dinosaur** this way.

The herd

The **fossils** of more than twenty Iguanodon have been found close together. This shows the animals lived in **herds**. Perhaps the fossils belong to a herd of Iguanodon that was drowned in a flood.

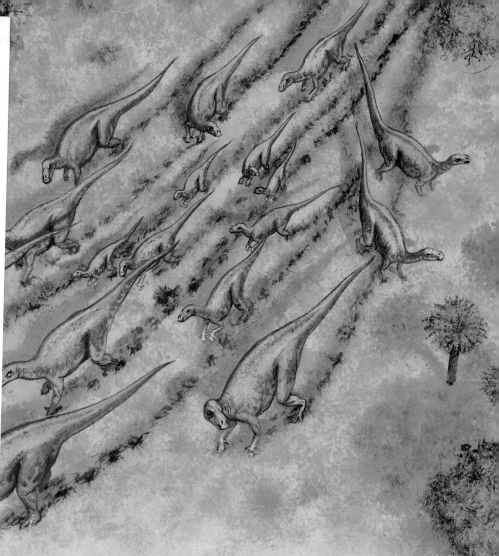

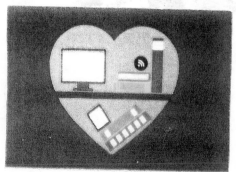

nk herds of Iguanodon kept close
safety. The adult animals may have
g on the outside of the herd. They could
hers if a meat-eating **dinosaur** was
e smaller Iguanodon stayed in the
e herd where it was safer.

23

Time to eat

Iguanodon had unusual **jaws**. At the front of the jaws was a sharp **beak**. The back of the jaws were full of strong, flat teeth. Iguanodon could move its upper jaw from side to side.

beak

Iguanodon jaws

Iguanodon used its beak to bite leaves and twigs from plants. Then it used its jaws to move the teeth from side to side. This ground up the plants into a thick paste. This paste could be **digested** quickly after it was swallowed.

Fighting Iguanodon

Iguanodon could use its front feet as weapons. Its thumb was a long and very sharp bony spike. The spike was covered in horn. This spike stuck out sideways from the wrist.

thumb spike

Iguanodon may have used its spike to defend itself against meat-eating **dinosaurs**. Iguanodon could jerk its front leg forwards using its strong **muscles**. This would jab the thumb spike into any meat-eating dinosaur that attacked.

Iguanodon around the world

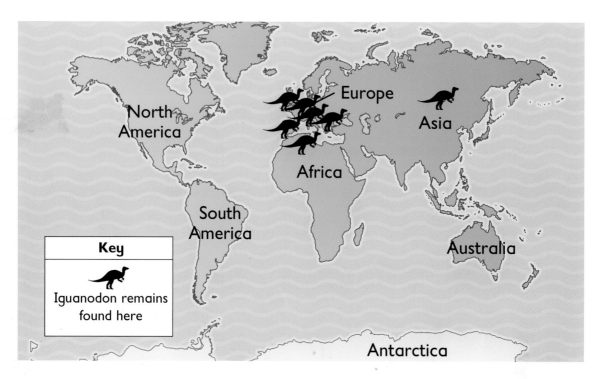

Key

Iguanodon remains found here

The **fossils** of Iguanodon have been found in different parts of Europe, Asia and in North Africa. The fossils of similar animals have been found in North America and China.

When did Iguanodon live?

Iguanodon lived on Earth between 125 and 100 million years ago (mya). It lived in the Age of the **Dinosaurs**, which scientists call the Mesozoic Era. This was in the early part of what scientists call the Cretaceous Period.

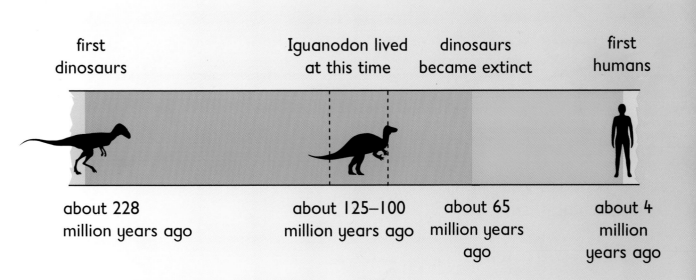

first dinosaurs	Iguanodon lived at this time	dinosaurs became extinct	first humans
about 228 million years ago	about 125–100 million years ago	about 65 million years ago	about 4 million years ago

Fact file

Iguanodon fact file	
Length:	up to 10 metres
Height:	up to 4 metres
Weight:	about 5 tonnes
Time:	Early Cretaceous Period, about 120 million years ago
Place:	Europe, Asia and North Africa

How to say it

Iguanodon – igg-wan-oh-don
dinosaur – dine-oh-saw
Polacanthus – pole-ah-kan-thus

Glossary

armour hard covering of shell or bone to protect soft body parts

beak hard, horny covering on jaws. Birds have beaks.

digested food that has been broken down into little pieces so it can be used by the body

dinosaurs reptiles that lived on Earth between 228 and 65 million years ago. Dinosaurs are extinct.

energy power to do things. Animals get this from food.

extinct an animal is extinct when there are none left alive

fossils remains of a plant or animal, usually found in rocks

geologist scientist who studies rocks

hatch when a baby animal breaks out of an egg

herd group of animals that live together

hind back legs or feet of an animal

hooves pieces of horn on the toes of some animals

jaw bones in the skull that hold the teeth

marsh area of ground that is very wet and muddy for most of the time

muscles parts in an animal's body that provide power to make it move

muscular having lots of muscles

palaeontologist scientist who studies fossils to discover about extinct animals, such as dinosaurs

valley low area of land between hills or mountains

Find out more

These are some other books about dinosaurs:
Iguanodon – Then and Now, K.S. Rodriguez (Raintree, 2000)
Big Book of Dinosaurs, Angela Wilkes (Dorling Kindersley, 1994)
Dinosaur Park, Nick Denchfield (Macmillan, 1998)

Look on these websites for more information:
www.bbc.co.uk/dinosaurs/fact_files/
www.cbv.ns.ca/marigold/history/dinosaurs/datafiles/iguanodon.html
www.oink.demon.co.uk/topics/dinosaur.htm

Index

Titles in the *Gone Forever* series include:

Hardback	0 431 16604 8

Hardback	0 431 16616 1

Hardback	0 431 16602 1

Hardback	0 431 16605 6

Hardback	0 431 16614 5

Hardback	0 431 16601 3

Hardback	0 431 16600 5

Hardback	0 431 16615 3

Hardback	0 431 16603 X

Find out about the other titles in this series on our website www.heinemann.co.uk/library